WHEN THE MEAT LOAF EXPLODES

IT'S DONE!

and other humorous recipes from life

MARTHA BOLTON

Beacon Hill Press of Kansas City
Kansas City, Missouri

10   9   8   7   6   5   4   3   2   1

To Bob and Diantha Ain,
who so unselfishly share
their love,
their talents,
and their joy with others.

CONTENTS

PREFACE

The Bible says in Prov. 15:15, "The cheerful heart has a continual feast" (NIV).

These days, it's not easy to keep a sense of humor. Every morning our newspapers are filled with gloom, doom, and senseless acts of violence. And once you get past the comics, things get even worse.

Still, God's Word is right. Maintaining a positive attitude is the best way to cope with life's problems—the little ones as well as the big ones.

A positive attitude will have you sleeping peacefully on those nights when your husband takes all the blankets and lies there dozin' while you're frozen.

It'll help you smile when, after two years of determined effort, you discover your savings account has barely topped the $12.00 mark.

And when you find out your three-year-old has been using your new golf club as a speed bump for her tricycle, a positive outlook will help you see the humor in that situation too—maybe not right away, but at least sometime before she gets married.

In other words, the choice is ours. We can spend our lives picking over a plate of sour grapes and lemons, or we can do what the Bible recommends and daily feast at the banquet of laughter and joy.

ACKNOWLEDGMENTS

A special thank-you to:

My husband, Russ, who has actually seen my meat loaf explode and lived to tell about it.

My eldest son, Rusty, who loves to see me working at my typewriter. It means the telephone's free.

My middle son, Matt, for all those times he practiced his drums while I was on deadline. (Matt, I just want to say that when I grow old and move in with you and your wife, I'm taking up the tuba!—just kidding, Matt. Your *father's* taking up the tuba. I'm buying a *bagpipe*.)

My youngest son, Tony, who tries his best to keep quiet and not interrupt me . . . especially when I'm counting out his allowance.

And finally, to all of you who have written to say how much you enjoy my books (OK, to the one lady in Des Moines who wrote), I appreciate your support.

"Something tells me we never should have bought those discount airline tickets."

▸▸▸ 1 ◂◂◂

THE "PROMISE" LAND

One of the most frightening moments of my life came while on a flight from St. Louis to Los Angeles. After barely one hour in the air, we encountered severe turbulence. I'm not saying how bumpy things got, but when I added cream and sugar to my coffee, it mixed itself.

I tried my best not to panic or make a scene. Even when the stewardess asked that I climb down off the lap of the lady next to me and sit in my own seat, I took it like an adult. Real fear didn't set in until the plane hit an air pocket, plunged several hundred feet, and forgot to take my stomach with it.

Immediately, the "Fasten Seatbelt" sign lit up, and the pilot asked all flight attendants to take their seats.

I tried taking my mind off the situation by putting on my earphones and listening to the in-flight entertainment. Unfortunately, the song they were playing was "Please Help Me—I'm Falling" and, needless to say, offered little consolation.

The turbulence grew steadily worse. I could hardly breathe as the plane was being tossed about—first to the right, then to the left. It wasn't long before the pilot made another announcement.

"We seem to be passing through some unstable air, folks," he explained in a calm, soothing voice. "Please stay in your seats and remain calm."

I wanted to remain calm, but it's not easy when the flight attendant is walking up and down the aisle saying, "Pillow? Blanket? Parachute?"

The lady next to me wasn't much help either. She kept asking the head flight attendant if our crashing would affect her frequent-flyer mileage in any way.

As the plane struggled to regain its altitude, I managed to pry my fingernails out of my armrest and reach for the emergency instruction brochure. I had heard those instructions plenty of times before, but now, in a real emergency, I couldn't remember if it was the seat cushion that doubles as a flotation device or the dinner roll from our lunch trays.

The plane continued its struggle against the strong

winds. I tightened my seatbelt, grabbed the airsickness bag from the pouch in front of me, and began penning my last will and testament on it. While I struggled to decide who'd get my recipe books (at that moment I couldn't think of anyone I disliked that much), the plane hit a second air pocket and plummeted another several hundred feet. In a situation like this, there was only one thing left for me to do. It's what many people do when faced with a life-or-death crisis. I started making promises to God.

"Lord," I prayed, "if You'll just get me out of this alive, I promise I'll do whatever You want me to do."

The plane began to shake, so I figured it was time to be a bit more specific.

"I'll attend church every single Sunday," I vowed.

The wing on my side of the plane began to vibrate.

"OK, throw in Wednesday night services too."

Lightning flashed and the plane veered off to the right.

"Did I mention increasing my tithe?"

One of the engines made a strange noise.

"I'll serve on the church visitation committee."

The noise grew louder.

"I'll help with the church newsletter too."

Another bolt of lightning flashed, and we began losing altitude.

"All right, all right!" I cried. "I'll teach children's church!"

Suddenly the turbulence eased, the plane leveled off, and the rest of the flight was calm and peaceful. The pilot thanked us for our cooperation, and the flight attendant assured me it was now safe to get off my knees.

When we finally landed, I was the second one to deplane. (The pilot was first.) Even through all of her smog, Los Angeles never looked so good.

I'm sure most of us have been in situations like this—situations that looked so frightening and hopeless, we vowed anything and everything to God. There's one thing we should remember, though—when the storm passes, our promises shouldn't go with it.

Mr. Simpleton makes the unfortunate mistake of asking for his savings account balance.

»»2«««

A PENNY SAVED . . .

In these uncertain economic times, it's not easy to save money. It's hard enough to remember what it looks like, much less save any of it.

My piggy bank gets fed so infrequently its ribs are starting to show, and lately the only thing you'll find hidden between my mattresses is dust.

In my younger days I was a far more disciplined saver. I actually managed to keep an active savings account for six years once. Unfortunately, though, the day came when I had to close it out. I needed the dollar.

It's important for every family to have a sound savings plan, especially for those unexpected household expenses that arise. I don't know about you, but I've noticed a direct correlation between the breakdown of a major household appliance and the amount of money my husband and I have in our savings account. If our passbook indicates a large enough balance to cover the average repair bill, the appliance will operate problem-free indefinitely. However, if we've managed to save only enough for a down payment on three screws and a fanbelt, the appliance will break down faster than we can say, "Those repairs are going to run us *what* an hour?"

My husband says my biggest problem with saving is that I can't seem to leave the money alone once it's been deposited.

"The bank pays interest by the day, Dear, not by the hour," he commented the other morning while glancing over our account statement. "If I make a deposit at noon and you withdraw it at 2 P.M., we haven't really gotten anywhere, have we?"

"We're getting to know all the bank tellers on a first-name basis," I pointed out. Without blinking, he continued.

"It says here that you took out $100 on the fifth, $65.00 on the sixth, and another $80.00 on the seventh. Thanks to you, our savings account has been seeing more takeouts than a Chinese restaurant."

"You're saying you don't like me dipping into our savings?" I asked, ever-so-innocently.

"You don't dip into our savings, Love Blossom—you *high-dive* into them!" He took a breath, then pressed on. "Look, the economy's in bad shape right now. Don't you realize we're living with a trillion-dollar debt?"

I gasped. "A trillion dollars? I had no idea our credit card limits were that high."

"I'm talking about the government deficit," he clarified. "We simply must start saving religiously."

"But we're already saving religiously," I pointed out.

"How do you figure that?" he asked.

"Every time I make a withdrawal, the teller tells me our savings account doesn't have a prayer."

I suppose when you get right down to it, the best savings plan is still the one recommended by our Lord some 2,000 years ago. Jesus said, "Lay up for yourselves treasures in heaven" (Matt. 6:20).

Pretty good advice, don't you think? After all, we're talking about heaven—the safest S and L around!

"On second thought, maybe you shouldn't sing to them."

»»3««

PARDON MY GARDEN

When it comes to my gardening skills, here's the dirt—my plants have spent less time in the green than the national budget! The only thing my clinging vine clings to is its life, and I'm one of the few people in the world who can grow her own dried flower arrangements.

The only plant I've successfully nurtured was a cactus. But that was easy. Its arms were already raised in surrender.

I've turned evergreens into "usually browns" and am a bigger threat to citrus trees than the Mediterranean fruit fly. Rumor has it that even the weeping willow didn't start weeping until I tried growing one.

None of my friends trust me to plant-sit for them. They realize that any plant left in my care will wilt within a two-hour period. That's if it's plastic. Live ones don't last even that long.

I'm the complete opposite of my father. His thumb was so green that everything he touched blossomed and thrived. He could spit orange seeds onto the ground, and there'd be an orchard growing there within weeks.

Dad knew my gardening skills were enough to make a Chia Pet run away; still he always tried his best to find something positive to say about my endeavors.

"Your cucumbers are coming in nicely," he noted one afternoon while looking over my vegetable patch. "They're a little on the small side, but their color's good."

Normally I would have been flattered at such a compliment, but he was pointing to my watermelons!

Whenever he could, Dad would offer free gardening tips too—like the time he said, "I think you're giving that plant a little too much sun."

"What makes you say that, Dad?" I asked.

"Well, for one thing, I've never seen a tulip with tan lines before."

Yes, Dad knew everything there was to know about gardening, but despite his noble efforts to share that knowledge with me, my thumb didn't turn any greener.

Hopefully, Dad's other lessons fell on more fertile

soil—lessons like how to pray, how to trust in the Lord, and how to look at life with a sense of humor. You can check with any nursery around, and you won't find any better seeds to plant in someone's heart.

"I fixed the dishwasher, Dear."

»»4««

HONEY-DOS AND HONEY-DON'TS

There are two ways to guarantee the death of an appliance at our house. One was is to allow its warranty to expire. The other is to let my husband fix it.

My husband loves to "fix" things. It doesn't matter if they're big, little, expensive, or inexpensive. It doesn't even matter if they need fixing. He works on everything in the house. Unfortunately, most of his repairs end up costing three times more than a legitimate repairman. (Four times more if it's just a simple repair.)

First, there was the refrigerator with the hum in it. A repairman quoted us $55.00 to fix it. In a effort to save money, though, my husband decided to do the repairs himself. Two hours and only $300 later, you could no longer hear the hum. The explosion drowned it out.

Then there was the time he tried fixing our automatic garage door opener. He worked an entire Saturday on it. It was a partial success. By that I mean it still won't open the garage door, but it will turn on our rear sprinklers and reprogram our neighbor's VCR.

He didn't do a very good job on our garbage disposal either. Ever since he worked on it, it's been refusing to swallow any of my cooking. (I get that from my family—I don't need it from an appliance.)

I'm not saying what happened when he tried fixing the leaks in our roof, but whenever it rains now, we can take a shower at 14 different locations in the house.

The household job he's most proud of was when he put new handles on all our kitchen cupboards. I have to admit they're beautiful and a perfect match to the woodwork. I just wish he would have put them on the *outside* of the cabinet doors.

Repairing our toaster presented some challenges for him. It was shooting toast up to the ceiling, so he figured it merely needed a simple adjustment. He made that adjustment. Now it propels the toast so far that NASA has to be notified.

Last week it was our vacuum cleaner's turn. He felt it needed more power, so he made another adjustment. It picks up everything now. When I emptied the bag I found socks, toys, two throw rugs, my old purse, and one wheezing but very grateful neighborhood cat.

I'm happy to report that one of his repairs did turn out for the better. That was when he repaired our front yard sprinklers. He worked on them eight hours, busted three water lines, and spent $850. They still don't work, but with that beautiful new lake in our front yard, who needs sprinklers?

Isn't it comforting to know that when God fixes the broken parts of our lives, He does it right the first time?

"Uh, Dear . . . I know this recipe is supposed to be cooked over a medium flame, but I don't think they meant **inside** the pan."

5

WHEN THE MEAT LOAF EXPLODES, IT'S DONE!

In the kitchen, timing is everything. Yet knowing when something is done has always been a problem for me. Is the roast done when it first becomes tender or when the neighbors rush in and start hosing it down? And what's the rule of thumb for pizza? I know it's done when something has melted, but I can never remember if it's the cheese or the pan.

From meat loaf to corn bread, from pudding to ham, you name it and I've either scorched it or torched it. Step 5 in most of my recipes is "Call 911," so it's no wonder on one recent Christmas morning my family lovingly presented me with a sign to put above my kitchen stove that says "Martha's Burn Center."

Someone suggested I use a timer when I cook. I gave this a try the other day, and I'm really glad I did. Now I know precisely how long it takes for a turkey to disintegrate in my oven.

A cake is supposed to be easy to time. You simply insert a knife into the middle of it. If the knife comes out clean, the cake is done. I very seldom use this method because of safety considerations. It's far too easy to burn myself while hammering in the knife.

Steak is my biggest challenge. No matter how hard I try, it seems I can prepare it only one of three ways: well-done, extremely well-done, and Steak Chernobyl.

Timing food in the microwave is another lost cause. I've caused brownies to self-flambé, potatoes to have a meltdown, and once my lasagna actually glowed for three weeks.

Don't think that overcooking is my only problem with timing. I recall a time I served some lamb that was so undercooked it started grazing in the salad. Bacon is something I have trouble timing too. I'm not saying how I usually serve it, but if it were any less done, the pig would still be wearing it.

My timing problems even go beyond the kitchen. I've left facial masks on so long they've had to be chiseled off. Home permanents present a challenge for me also. I forgot one once and left it on my hair for three hours and 45 minutes. Luckily, my hair didn't fall out, but it ended up with a tighter curl than a Slinky.

I'll never forget the summer I failed to set the timer on my sunlamp. Without going into all the details about how I turned out, suffice it to say we didn't have to use any lighting in our house for a month.

Aren't you glad God's timing is perfect? He knows what's best for us exactly *when* it's best for us. There's no guesswork to His will, no trial and error to His plan. At times, our human nature grows impatient and we want to hurry things up, or we become fearful and try to slow things down. If only we could learn to trust our lives to His care and perfect timing, we could rest assured that everything will always turn out "just right."

"Sure, this house is built upon sand and will wash away in the slightest rainstorm, but think what it'll save you on moving expenses."

▶▶▶6◀◀◀

DIRT CHEAP

My husband and I have always dreamed of building our own home on a nice acre or two. Since real estate prices are good right now, we've begun shopping around for vacant land.

I have nothing against tract houses. It's just that some of the ones being built today have backyards that are so small a dog has to stand on his hind legs just to fit. And for this they charge a lot premium.

Frankly, we'd like a little more elbow room than that. Finding a buildable lot in a good location, though, can be a difficult task—almost as difficult as finding the right real estate agent.

I knew someone in real estate. We had never met, but I had more things in my house personalized with her name than I had with my own. I called her the other day to tell her we were in the market for a buildable piece of property. She said she'd check through her multiple listings and get back to me.

As I hung up the telephone, there was a knock at the door. It was her. Handing me her business card and a dozen or so note pads, she introduced herself.

"I recognize you from the 8-by-10 you left last week," I said, inviting her in, "and from the poster you gave out at Christmas."

"The murals will be here Easter," she assured me, then went on to describe the "perfect" lot she had found for us.

"It's just what you want—a private driveway, plenty of seclusion, your own little valley."

It sounded ideal, so grabbing my coat and purse, I agreed to go with her to look at it.

As we drove into the hills, we passed several beautifully level lots with breathtaking views.

"Is it one of these?" I asked excitedly.

"Not in your price range," she noted without slowing down a beat.

The next lots we came to weren't quite as level, but still appeared buildable.

"How about one of these?" I asked curiously.

"Were you shopping for yourself or Ross Perot?" she cracked. "Those are way out of your league. The one I'm taking you to is perfect. Trust me."

After driving another half-hour, I noticed the scenery beginning to change remarkably. The grass became weeds, the trees became dead stumps, the paved roads became dirt ones. We zigzagged around tumbleweeds and boulders for another 10 minutes before she finally pulled over and parked.

"We'll have to take a burro the rest of the way," she said, exiting the car.

"Isn't this a little remote?" I asked, unimpressed.

"I thought you said you wanted a private driveway," she countered.

"I did," I replied. "But not 26 miles long."

She didn't comment. She merely handed me another business card. This one was laminated.

"By the way," she smirked, "I was just kidding about the burro. We'll have to *walk* the rest of the way."

Sensing my hesitation, she added, "It'll be worth it. Trust me."

It wasn't. After a 15-minute hike, she finally stopped and pointed off to the right.

"Well, what do you think?" she beamed.

I turned to look at my dream lot.

"Well," she persisted, handing me several more business cards for my friends.

"When you said I'd have my own valley, I had no idea it'd be within the lot itself. How deep is that hole?" my voice echoed.

"Don't think of it as a hole," she smiled, slyly. "Think of it as the perfect location for your sunken living room."

"Most sunken living rooms don't drop two stories," I quipped. "Are you sure a meteorite didn't fall here?"

"That's even better," she exclaimed. "Those things almost never fall in the same place *twice*. That should take a real load off your mind."

She began pacing off the lot, but each time the wind changed, so did the legal description. I didn't need to see any more. I turned and started walking toward the car. It was obvious I was going to have to keep shopping around for a good lot—and maybe another real estate agent too. After all, a house, like a life, is only as strong as what it's built upon.

"Ah, finally—a street without any traffic."

▶▶▶ 7 ◀◀◀

DRIVING, MISSED DAISY . . . AND THE STREETLIGHT, AND THE FIRE HYDRANT, AND . . .

On her 70th birthday my mother received an impressive 100 on her written driving test. 100! Obviously, I did not inherit her driving talents.

Don't get me wrong. I have a fair behind-the-wheel record. I never make unsafe lane changes. When I'm driving the wrong direction down a one-way street, the other drivers usually yield and allow me to make whatever lane changes I want. I don't even tailgate other cars. (Although I'll admit a few have towed me without their knowledge.) I yield to pedestrians too. I know they were on the sidewalk first.

But even with skills like these, I've yet to garner a perfect score on a Department of Motor Vehicles exam. The primary reason for this is that I find D.M.V. questions a little tricky, questions like—

"If you hear a fire engine behind you, should you speed up and get out of its way or slow down and pull over to the right?"

My answer is "Neither. I'd simply let him follow me to my house, then help him put out the pot roast."

Questions about street signs are equally hard to answer. For instance, what does "Ped Xing" mean? Obviously, it means someone flunked spelling in school, but I don't think that's the answer they're looking for.

Or how about the question "What does a broken yellow line mean?" I'm not sure what it means in the rest of the country, but in California it means we just had another aftershock.

Questions about parking can be tricky, but it's important that every driver have a good understanding of parking rules. L.A. drivers especially need to know how to park. It's a skill that comes in handy on our freeways during rush hour.

"What does it mean when you see a curb painted green?" is another question I seldom get right. I figure it means my kids got into my art supplies, but that's marked wrong too.

The question I have the most trouble with is the one about when to report an accident. "Not until my husband's in a good mood" sounds right to me, but they've never given me credit for it.

Even with all its tricky questions, though, I'm determined to score 100 on my next driver's license exam. I'm going to study and study until I'm certain I can match my mother's perfect score—if not on the written or driving portions of the test, then at least on the eye exam. Now let's see—that was "First line—E; second line—F, T, S, Z; third line . . ."

The making of a volunteer.

»»8«««

THE ABSENTEE VOLUNTEER

I try never to miss a church planning meeting. Over the years I've learned that whatever job or position comes up, he who isn't there is the next volunteer. Miss one crucial meeting and you could find yourself the new youth camp counselor, director of the church remodeling committee, and the recipient of a lifetime teaching position for the kindergartners' Sunday School class.

Sometimes others volunteer you even when you *are* at the meetings. I've had my hand raised for me more often than a fighter after winning a boxing match.

Some of the jobs were things I might have volunteered for myself. Others weren't. Oddly enough, I usually enjoyed the latter more. It seemed the more unqualified I felt in a certain position, the more I had to lean on God.

A well-meaning church official once decided that I should be the one to lead the youth choral group. Imagine that. Me—a person who couldn't sing her way out of a paper bag. (I know I can't sing my way out of a paper bag, because that's what they always make me wear in choir.)

I accepted the challenge, though, and God took care of everything else. The youth were talented and terrific to work with. I think they knew I was in over my head, but they appreciated my willingness to help. They didn't even make me stand up and direct them the night of the performance. All I had to do was sit on the front row and mouth the words as they sang. (Mouthing the words was something else thay taught me to do in choir.)

One year my pastor volunteered me to write our annual Christmas play. I was working as church secretary at the time, and I guess he figured I'd seen enough comedy and drama to be able to pull it off. Again, I was inexperienced in this area, but I decided to give it a try anyway. As soon as I wrote the play, our pastor decided I should be the one to direct it as well. (I think he gave me both jobs so I'd be too busy to sing in the choir's Christmas cantata.) Whatever his reasoning, I'm glad he did it. The play was a success, the cast had a good time, and through that experience I discovered that church drama was where my heart is.

So whether you're the one volunteering or someone's volunteering you, the Lord can help you do things you never dreamed possible. Moses wasn't a public speaker; still God chose him to address Pharaoh. David was a mere boy, but God selected him to stand up to Goliath. And Sarah was 90 when God decided she should have a baby. (That was her first miracle. Her second was when God helped a 103-year-old mother survive the teenage years!)

In other words, if the job seems overwhelming, chances are you're just the person He has in mind for it.

"Just because we're camping, Dear, doesn't mean you shouldn't try to do something about morning breath."

▸▸▸9◂◂◂

AS A ROARING LION

There are many reasons why I don't enjoy camping. No room service, no television, no telephone, no fax machine, no complimentary shampoo, no daily maid service, no swimming pool, and no Jacuzzi are just eight of them. The main reason, though, occurred several years ago when my family talked me into visiting a campground just outside Los Angeles. They didn't actually *talk* me into it—they *tricked* me into it. They told me we were

going to a Sheraton. My husband said he was only bringing along the camping gear in the event they were
booked.

I could have forgiven them even for that, but what
they pulled at the campsite wasn't so easily pardoned.
After setting up our tent for the night, they did a very
cruel thing—perhaps the cruelest thing anyone could do
to a novice camper: They all feel asleep before me. All
night I had to sit there wide-eyed inside our tent trem-
bling at every single noise I heard. Was that a bear in the
trash? Was that a coyote sniffing around our tent? Why's
that lion growling so loudly?

Wait a minute. Did I say *lion*?

Frantically, I tried shaking my husband awake.

"Did you hear that?"

"Hear what?" he asked groggily.

"That," I whispered as yet another roar echoed
through the canyons. "There's a lion out there."

"A lion?—running around Los Angeles at two in the
morning?" he scoffed as he rolled over in his sleeping
bag. "Not even a lion's *that* brave."

He fell back to sleep, but it was only a temporary
rest, because before long I heard another roar, even louder than the first.

"There it is again," I gasped.

"There's *what* again?" he said, opening only one eye.

"The lion," I persisted.

"Just how many chili dogs did you eat for dinner
anyway?"

"I didn't eat *any* chili dogs. I heard a lion, I tell you.
Now wake up!"

"Ah, I get it. This is your little way of punishing me

for not taking you to a Sheraton. Well, it's not going to work," he stated flatly. "We're roughing it this weekend, and that's final! It was bad enough that you made me run an electrical line from the camp office to our tent for your typewriter and fax machine."

"I'm not trying to punish you, and I'm not making this up," I insisted. "There's a lion out there, and he doesn't sound very happy."

"I don't blame him," he grumbled. "Your talking's probably keeping him awake too. Now be quiet and let us both get some sleep."

OK, so I could understand him being a bit skeptical. He probably still remembered the time I called the police because I thought I heard a snake *walking* around in our cupboard. But what about all the other people at the campground? Surely they heard the roaring. It was obvious a lion had escaped from somewhere. Why wasn't someone calling the animal regulation department? the L.A. Zoo? MGM? Didn't they care that their lives were in danger?

The answer, of course, was no. The safety of my family now depended solely on me. I grabbed a frying pan and prepared to slam it down on the first wild thing that would dare pop its head through our tent door.

With my heart pounding and my palms sweating, I kept a constant vigil until morning. Then, at the first crack of dawn, I took a cautious glance around the campsite and ran to the campground office to warn the manager. When I told him about the growling, he merely laughed.

"Growling? You mean like lions?"

"You heard it too?" I said, finally feeling validated.

He nodded. "I apologize. They're usually not that noisy."

"You mean there's more than one?"

"Yeah, but they're caged," he winked. "There's a place up the road that has lions, elephants, all sorts of critters. Their owner rents them out to the movies."

Then, glancing into my bloodshot eyes, he smirked, "You didn't lose any sleep over a few caged lions, did you?"

I glared at him for a few moments, smiled weakly, then turned and walked away. He didn't want to hear about it.

I wonder, how many times have we lost sleep over one of life's "lions," only to find out it had been caged all along?

"I don't understand it, Dear. I'm pushing the 'eject' button, but the cassette tape just isn't coming out."

▸▸▸10◂◂◂

LOST IN THE LAP OF LUXURY

When Ray Bradbury agreed to speak at my writing club's annual banquet several years ago, I had no idea I'd get to be the one to chauffeur him. It seems he doesn't drive, so our club president asked my husband and me if we'd mind picking him up at his west Los Angeles home. Mind? I jumped at the chance. After all, I'd been following his career ever since I'd heard him speak at my junior high school. This was the chance of a lifetime. I'd now have the noted author all to myself for an hour each way—even longer if we had car trouble.

Imagine it—the one-and-only Ray Bradbury, author of *Fahrenheit 451, The Martian Chronicles,* and *The Illustrated Man,* sitting in my car. Of course, I'd have to wash it and perhaps even repaint it, and it did need a little body work, and . . . well, actually, the more I thought about it the harder it was to imagine the one-and-only Ray Bradbury sitting in *that* car. I was certain an author of Bradbury's worldwide reputation was used to riding in chauffeur-driven limousines. Somehow, picking him up in our aging subcompact seemed a little like serving caviar from a Baggie. It simply wasn't classy enough.

"Oh, come on, Martha—he's mortal just like the rest of us," insisted my husband when I tried talking him into selling our house and buying a new Jaguar for the event. "I'm sure Mr. Bradbury won't care what kind of car we drive. Anyway, you don't want to look pretentious."

"Of course I want to look pretentious," I countered. "I've always wanted to look pretentious, and this is my big chance. Besides, we could use the dealership's rebate to pay for our banquet tickets."

My logic made no sense to him, but it didn't matter because a good friend of ours, the owner of a beautiful new Cadillac, soon came to the rescue. He graciously offered to trade cars with us for the evening.

It was raining the night of the banquet, and we were running a little behind schedule when we arrived at our friend's home to switch vehicles. He handed us the keys and gave a quick rundown on how to operate the rows and rows of little buttons lining the dashboard. Likewise, I handed him our keys and explained how to operate our car.

"Insert the key in the ignition and pray."

With only 30 minutes to get to west L.A., we raced down the freeway. Before long the windows began to fog up.

"Do you remember which button he said would turn on the defrost?" my husband asked, wiping the windshield with his shirt sleeve.

I shook my head. "Maybe they're marked."

"It looks like they're all picture-coded," he said.

"Picture-coded? No one understands picture-coding," I moaned. "Life was so much simpler before everyone tried to simplify it."

Meanwhile, visibility inside the car was nearing zero, so in a panic I began pushing all the buttons in sight.

"Is it on yet?" I asked after hitting the first 20 buttons.

"No, but the air-conditioner is, and I think the trunk just flew open."

"I haven't tried this one yet," I said, reaching for yet another button.

"Don't touch that one," he snapped.

"Why not?"

"It opens the sunroof."

"How do you know that?" I asked, drawing back my hand.

"I pushed it earlier when I was trying to find the windshield wipers."

By now there were only three buttons left to try, so I pushed them all at once. The first two reclined each of our seats, and the third set off the security alarm.

Needless to say, it was an interesting trip. By the time we reached Ray Bradbury's home, we had somehow managed to turn off everything that was supposed to be turned off and turned on everything that was supposed to be turned on—everything, that is, except for the defroster. We never did find that button. I don't think he realized it, though. (OK, once on our way home he did comment on how cloudy it was, but I'm sure he was talking about *outside* the car, not *inside*.)

All in all, it was an evening I'll never forget. The Cadillac was luxurious, and I appreciated our friend letting us use it. Considering Ray Bradbury's status as a writer, it was good that we were able to pick him up in style. But considering his warm and unassuming personality, I have a feeling he would have enjoyed even our old family car.

I also learned something very important that night. If we're trying to be someone other than ourselves, chances are we're hitting all the wrong buttons.

"I can't believe we went all the way to Yellowstone and forgot to bring home a single souvenir."

▸▸▸ 11 ◂◂◂

YOU KNOW IT'S TIME TO GO HOME WHEN . . .

The annual family vacation can be a time of great fun, relaxation, and togetherness. However, you know it's time to go home when . . .

- Your car's radiator is keeping a more regular eruption schedule than Old Faithful.
- You can't remember at which rest stop you left your hat, your sunglasses, and two of your children.

- The magnetic pull of all your souvenir refrigerator magnets is starting to suck the bumpers off passing cars.
- You stop singing "Ain't We Got Fun?" and start singing "Show Me the Way to Go Home."
- You call home to get your messages, and your answering machine doesn't remember who you are.
- After 1,487 tries, you still haven't figured out how to refold your map.
- Your windshield has killed more unsuspecting flying insects than my leftovers.
- You don't know which is getting balder—your tires or the numbers on your American Express card.
- There's so much dirty laundry in your suitcases, buzzards are starting to circle your luggage rack.
- You're actually starting to like the hot dogs at gas station minimarts.
- You're finding the last of your cash is harder to hold onto than one of those tiny bars of motel soap.
- You've smiled and said "cheese" so often you feel like a Kraft salesman.
- Every time you open the trunk of your car, other tourists mistake it for a roadside souvenir store and start shopping.
- The mosquitoes are taking bigger bites out of you than the IRS.
- Your car's gathered more dust than your kids' school books.
- That irritating "Are we there yet?" whining is getting totally out of hand. But no matter how hard they try, your kids can't get you to stop doing it.

- You don't know which has more new bulges—your luggage or your waist.
- But you really know it's time to go home when your MasterCard, your VISA, and your nerves have all hit their limits.

»» 12 ««
SHOP AT HOME AND . . . SAVE?

Home parties usually come in waves. You won't hear of any for years, then all of a sudden you receive eight invitations in the same week—seven of them from people you haven't heard from since kindergarten.

While going to a home party may be fun, giving one is another matter entirely—for me, anyway. Few people show up at my home parties. The last one I gave was the worst. I cleaned the house, shampooed the carpets, burned six dozen chocolate chip cookies, then sat back and waited for all my excited guests to rush in, grab their order forms, and spend, spend, spend.

The dealer was the first to arrive.

"So how many invitations did you mail out?" she asked while setting up two folding tables in the middle of my living room.

"Fifty-eight," I replied, helping her drape a maroon cloth over the tables. "But some of those were to out-of-state friends. I doubt they'll come."

After arranging the merchandise in a calculated manner, we both anxiously awaited the onslaught of enthusiastic home shoppers.

The paperboy came by at 7:45. I tried talking him into staying, but he claimed he had more collections to make.

At 8:07 the telephone rang. It was a wrong number, but before hanging up I gave the lady on the line directions to my home and pleaded with her to join us. She said she'd try. Since that was the same promise I'd received from the gas man who'd read my meter earlier in the day and he hadn't showed up yet, I didn't get my hopes up.

The clock ticked on and I could sense the dealer getting more and more anxious. My mind, though, was totally focused on winning the food processor the company had advertised. It could be mine for a mere $300 in sales and two bookings.

"Is it true," I asked, trying to stimulate conversation, "if I have 12 or more guests come tonight, I'll get four bonus points?"

"Yes," she said, nervously tapping her watch. "But it's already nine o'clock. Are your friends always this late?"

"Perhaps they're having trouble parking," I said, glancing out the window.

"Well, you still get two bonus points for just having

the party," she said, trying to make me feel better.

"Really," I beamed. "And what will that get me?"

"This melon baller," she smiled, proudly displaying the plastic utensil.

The melon baller was useful, but I had my heart set on a food processor.

"Wait a minute," I interjected. "Outside orders count, don't they?"

As soon as she nodded, I ran into my bedroom and began filling out all the order forms included in my party planning kit. I'd intended on buying a few items myself anyway, so now I cleverly divided my order onto the different forms, using my married name, my maiden name, my nickname, and my cat's name.

I handed in the orders.

"Not bad," she said, only briefly raising an eyebrow when she got to "Fluffy's" order.

After a quick totaling of my sales, she excitedly announced I needed only 65 more dollars and two more bookings for the food processor to be mine.

Only $65.00 more! I quickly doubled Fluffy's order. I figured she was good for it. This pushed me well over the $300 mark.

It was now almost ten o'clock, and I was only two bookings away from earning my prize.

"You know, you can book off your own party," she coaxed, while packing away the merchandise. "Just have two more parties within the next month. You're so close to winning, don't give up now."

I thought for a moment. She was right. I was close. Besides, if I could sell $300 worth of merchandise to myself this easily at just one party, just think how much I could sell to myself at two more parties. Who knows—next time I might order $350 worth of merchandise! or $400! or $450! Why, with my shopping habits, I could order every item in the catalog and win all their prizes! I could bankrupt the company!

"Well," she persisted, polishing the food processor. "What do you say?"

"How does Tuesday the 12th and Thursday the 21st sound?" I asked excitedly.

She made the notations, handed me another stack of order forms, and wished me luck.

I didn't need luck. I had my checkbook. After only two more parties, I earned enough points for both the food processor *and* the melonballer. And to think they only cost me $2,486!

It's a good thing God's love isn't something I have to earn.

A typical closet **before** the wife clears out a space for her husband's clothes.

A typical closet **after** the wife clears out a space for her husband's clothes.

⯈⯈⯈13⯇⯇⯇

THE GREAT CLOSET TAKEOVER

Recently I came across an advertisement for custom closet organizers that read, "Save your marriage! Clear out the clutter in your closets!"

There's a lot of truth in that ad. Cluttered closets can place added stress on a marriage. I know. My husband went into our closet three years ago, and I haven't seen him since. (I'm exaggerating, of course. Our eldest son spotted him last week peering out from behind one of the boxes and holding up a white flag.)

The reason I have so much closet clutter is that I can't throw anything away. Some of the dresses hanging in my closet are so old even the moths are embarrassed to be seen in them. One dress dates all the way back to my high school days. If you're wondering if it still fits, let's just say the Democrats and Republicans have a greater chance of coming together than those buttons and buttonholes.

I have a difficult time parting with my old footwear as well. From worn-out running shoes to broken high heels, I've kept them all. Some of my shoes are so ancient the Odor-Eaters inside them have petrified.

Men seem to have an easier time when it comes to clearing out closets. My husband doesn't think twice about giving away boots with holes in the toes or slacks that are so old that if you pulled one thread, they'd unravel faster than the U.S.S.R. For some reason, men don't seem to get as attached to their possessions as women do. (I think it's a trait they've developed from years of losing their golf balls.)

Beyond the clutter, there's another reason closets can be hard on a marriage. In most marriages, things are shared evenly. This applies to everything except the closet. A woman can have her own walk-in closet the size of Montana and still insist she needs half of her husband's broom closet!

I haven't tested this theory, but I think there may be a direct correlation between how long a couple has been married and how much of the closet the man of the house has left.

The other day my husband pointed out (once again) that he wasn't getting his fair share of the closet space.

"But, Dear," I insisted, "I've divided our closet exactly 50-50."

"I know," he said. "Fifty percent for your summer apparel and 50 percent for your winter apparel."

"And your point is . . . ?" I pressed, not fully understanding where he was headed.

"My point is—where am I supposed to hang *my* clothes? Don't get me wrong. I love that tie rack you bought me for Father's Day, but my suits keep falling off it."

Men, I thought to myself. They're never satisfied, are they? Besides, he was overstating his plight. He had more closet space than just that tie rack. He had a belt organizer too. That alone could easily hold four or five of his dress shirts.

I started to remind him of that fact but ultimately decided against it. In my heart, I knew both he and the ad were probably right. I really should organize our closet and give him back his rightful share.

But first I'm looking into squatter's rights!

"Yessir, you won't find a more fuel-efficient car than this one."

»14«

SMALL PROBLEMS

The other day I went shopping for a new car. I told the salesman I wanted a small, inexpensive, fuel-efficient vehicle—just a little something to get me around town. He assured me he had the exact one I needed. It wasn't in the showroom, of course. They save that for the "real" cars. To see my vehicle, we had to walk behind the dealership, down the embankment, and over the extension bridge to the rear parking lot.

Grabbing a set of car keys and giving a quick "get-out-the-contract" wink to his manager, the salesman began leading me to what was sure to be the car of my dreams.

"Well, what do you think?" he asked when we finally came to a little blue car that barely came to my waist.

"You're kidding, aren't you?" I said, aiming my breath away from the vehicle so it wouldn't tip over in the breeze. "Tonka makes bigger cars than this."

"It gets great gas mileage," he continued, undaunted.

"So does a skateboard," I cracked. Luckily, my kids weren't with me, or they would have tried putting a quarter in it for a ride.

"This car couldn't possibly keep up with the flow of traffic," I remarked, unimpressed.

"Lady," he said, "we're in Los Angeles. Everyone knows traffic doesn't flow here."

He had a point, but I still wasn't sold. I began asking about extras.

"Does it have air-conditioning?"

"You bet," he beamed. "Low, medium, and high, depending on how far down you roll the windows."

"What about cruise control?"

"As long as this baby's in neutral and headed downhill, it'll cruise for hours," he assured me.

"And what's this?" I asked, opening a cute little door. "The glove compartment?"

"No—the trunk."

"It's not very big," I whined. "Where's the spare tire?"

"It's there," he insisted. "In the envelope."

"How about the seats?" I asked. "Do they recline?"

"Absolutely," he said, then demonstrated by breaking the release on the passenger seat. "Getting them back up, though, can be a bit of a trick. So what do you say? You want to take it out for a test run?"

"Will we have to stay in the slow lane?" I asked, with just a hint of sarcasm.

"Drive where you normally drive," he said, confidently.

I shook my head. "I'd probably get stuck in all those lawns."

He assured me that I could indeed drive it over lawns as well as on streets, and so, after a hearty push, we were off.

To my surprise, it didn't start giving us trouble until we had done, oh, at least 10 or 20 feet.

"It probably just needs to warm up," the salesman apologized.

"But the temperature gauge indicates it's overheating now."

"That's only until we get over this hill."

"You mean this speed bump," I corrected.

"One car's speed bump is another car's Mount Everest," he snapped. "Now, c'mon, we're almost to the top. Lean forward! Lean forward!"

After the hour-long test drive (we never did get out of the parking lot), the salesman was absolutely convinced he had a sale. I had to disappoint him, though. After all, a car is a major investment. I had to be sure. Besides, I hadn't even checked out what Mattel had to offer yet.

Aren't you glad God's promises are exactly what they appear to be?

"Take two aspirin and fax me in the morning."

»»15««

THE MALADY SUPERBOWL

Have you ever asked someone how he was and found yourself regretting it the minute he began listing every malady he's endured for the past 46 years?

Personally, I think I've heard more firsthand accounts of injuries, illnesses, and surgical procedures in the frozen-food aisle at our local grocery store than my doctor has in his consultation office.

Take, for example, the lady I met this week who not only told me every last detail of her latest operation, but insisted on showing me her four-and-a-half-inch incision right there by the Stouffer's display.

Then, there was a gentleman I sat next to at a banquet once. I should have known I was in for it when I noticed that his Medic-Alert bracelet stated, "See accompanying four-volume medical diary." He answered my "How are you?" with a 30-minute update on his five-year-old abdominal surgery. He knew it had been five years since the operation because he sends anniversary cards to his surgeon.

I tried acting interested. After all, *any* surgery is serious. But when he started to analyze the pros and cons of drainage tubes, I had to stop him. Banquet food is hard enough to digest with dinner music only, much less a stitch-by-stitch account of someone's surgery.

Then there are the "souvenir collectors." Souvenir collectors are people who save all sorts of medical and surgical paraphernalia, then insist on showing you their collections every time you see them. These collections can include used bandages, old stitches, laminated operative reports, or framed 12-by-16 X rays of themselves.

Sometimes a souvenir collector will even get creative. I heard of one guy who had his gallstones made into a mosaic, then hung it over his fireplace. Another lady fashioned hers into an earring. (She's now awaiting a second surgery so she can have a matched set.) Yet another man had Christmas cards made out of his MRI images, and created a necklace for his wife out of his old IV tubing.

The absolute worst, though, is the "malady topper." No matter what you've had, he's had it worse. His flu was the most severe and only one of its kind (he explains this while sneezing on you). If your surgery lasted four hours, his went through the weekend. If your temperature was 103 degrees, his set the blanket on fire.

Frankly, I've never understood malady toppers. Who wants to win at such a depressing game? That's why I refuse to participate in their Malady Superbowl. I *already* know my surgery was worse than theirs, and their bouts with the flu couldn't possibly have been as devastating as mine. But you won't see me stopping everyone I meet on the street and boring them with all the sordid details. I realize people today just don't have the time to stand there and listen to my medical horror stories and tales of surgical woes.

That's why I'm having the fliers printed up.

"I know that, Mom."

"Now remember, this is a big store. Stay right by my side and you won't get lost."

"I **was talking** to your father."

➤➤16◀◀
"HUSBAND LOST IN SHOPPING MALL! CALL $9.11!"

I lost my husband last week. It's not what you think though. He didn't pass away. I really *did* lose him. Allow me to explain.

We were shopping in a mall and somehow became

separated. (I think I saw a half-price sale three stores away and he just couldn't keep up.)

You may not be aware of this, but a lot of men have no sense of direction in a mall. They often get lost and aren't sure how to find their way out. In extreme emergencies, some malls will page the wife, announcing that her husband has been located and where she might pick him up. Such an announcement isn't always a good idea, however, since the wife may be tempted to take advantage of the situation and first complete her shopping. I heard of one lady who lost her husband in a mall during the Christmas shopping season and didn't show up to claim him until after the Presidents' Day Sale in February.

The primary reason men become M.I.M.s (Missing In Malls) is a simple one: They don't mentally register landmarks the way women do. Women can easily recall that they entered through the sportswear section, turned left at purses and accessories, then doubled back through evening wear before hanging a right at petites. To men, all these departments look alike, so it's no wonder they end up walking in more circles than Joshua did at the battle of Jericho.

For basic mall survival, a husband needs to make his own mental log of the journey. He needs to remember he turned left at the coat rack where his wife tried on that $200 jacket and his checkbook started hyperventilating, then turned right at the jewelry counter where the salesman knew her charge number by heart, and finally circled back through the furniture department where he took that brief nap on the marble coffee table.

No matter how many times I've urged him, though, remembering mall landmarks is a skill my husband has never quite mastered. So as soon as I realized he was missing that day, I did the only thing I could do: I tried on five or six more outfits and then notified security.

It was only 11 A.M., but the security guard said my husband was already the third missing husband of the day. Making no promises, he took the report and quickly organized a search party, complete with specially trained husband-sniffing dogs. I thanked him and said that if he needed me, I'd be in housewares for their month-end clearance sale.

The first hour passed without a word on my husband's whereabouts. I made my purchases, then moved on to the next department. A second hour passed, then a third.

After four long hours (I was able to squeeze in the two-for-one sale in linens too), someone reported seeing smoke signals coming from the tool department. I knew it had to be him. All the other lost husbands were sending up flares, and I was sure he'd want to be different.

Hurriedly, I finished going through the last three sale bins, then rushed to his side. (I had reached my credit limit anyway.)

It was a touching reunion. He cried so many tears of joy, he rusted two boxes of nails. As a matter of fact, he was so happy to see me that he didn't even mind carrying my 14 packages, six shoe boxes, and matching wingback chairs.

As happy as we were to have found each other, though, our trial was only half over. It was time now for the most difficult and daring search of all to begin. It was time to start looking for our car in the mall parking lot!

»17«

GOING NOWHERE FAST

Have you ever been trapped in an elevator? It's not something I'd recommend. There's not a lot to do in there, and after a couple of hours the music can really get on your nerves. I know this from firsthand experience.

Actually, I should have realized this particular elevator was dangerous when it dropped me off nine inches shy of the eighth floor. This, and the fact that it tended to swing whenever someone stepped into it, should have been enough warning for me to take the stairs. But I'm a trusting soul.

Once I had finished my business on the eighth floor, I walked back to the elevator, pushed the "down" button, and waited patiently for it to arrive. I waited and I waited and I waited.

Finally, after five minutes passed, I gave up and decided taking the stairs would be faster. The minute I reached the stairwell, though, the elevator came. I rushed back to catch it, but by the time I got there it was gone.

Once again, I pressed the "down" button and waited. After another five minutes and no sign of the elevator, I made my way to the stairs once more. As soon as I reached them, the elevator returned. I raced back but wasn't quick enough.

This little game continued until I finally wised up and only *pretended* to head for the stairs. Instead, I hid behind the drinking fountain. When the elevator came this time, I was ready. I ran to it, wedged my foot between the doors, and squeezed through.

Inside, the elevator was quite crowded. A quick estimate of the combined weight of everyone on board drove me to one simple conclusion—it was a good thing we were going down.

When we stopped at the seventh floor, five more people made their way on. That wouldn't have been so bad, but three of them were pushing strollers.

One floor later, the guy in the rear with the mail cart expressed a desire to exit. No one could move, though, so he missed his floor. Maybe rain and snow can't keep a mailman from his appointed rounds, but a crowded elevator is another story.

It was between the fourth and fifth floors that the

elevator decided to stop. Thinking quickly, I picked up the emergency telephone and called for help. Once assured that help was on its way, I figured I'd take advantage of the situation and make a few more phone calls. After all, with three teenagers in the house, it was the first time in months I'd been able to get near a telephone.

The others, hysterical and fearing we might all starve to death by the time help arrived, began checking through their pockets and purses for emergency rations. All that turned up, however, was one lint-covered sucker and a half-eaten chocolate bar that appeared to have started a life of its own.

Finally, after what seemed like an eternity, the elevator started moving again. The people cheered, they cried, they began hugging each other in a fit of uncontrollable joy and relief. I'm sure I would have joined them, too, but I still had a few more calls to make.

Whatever has you stalled isn't important. The only thing that matters is that you get moving again.

"Did you beep me, Mom?"

»»18««

THE PARENT OLYMPICS

Have you noticed how competitive the world of parenting has become? It used to be that you simply had to contend with the inevitable one-upmanship of other proud parents. If your son was talking by the age of six months, theirs was giving corporate speeches. If your daughter was walking at eight months, theirs was pole-vaulting into her high chair. And if your little genius could count to 10 by his first birthday, theirs had found a way to erase the national debt without raising taxes, lowering government spending, or auctioning off the Grand Canyon.

Today the competition is even more fierce. Some parents are determined to raise the smartest, strongest, cutest baby around, and they'll do anything and everything to achieve that goal.

They install fax machines in their children's playpens, cellular phones on their strollers, and give them subscriptions to pop-up versions of *Money* and *The Wall Street Journal*. They fasten their diapers with money clips and read Mother Goose to them in six languages—English, Spanish, French, German, Latin, and rap.

Then there are the classes. They enroll their toddlers in such offerings as "Sandbox Archaeology" and "Mommy and Me Calculus." Gone are the days of mere swimming lessons for toddlers. Nowadays the child is considered deprived if he doesn't know how to scuba, snorkel, and surf before his third birthday.

It's easy to get caught up in this competition. Society makes us feel guilty if our children aren't on the lecture circuit by the time they can hold a Mr. Microphone. I mean, let's face it: when's the last time you saw a bumper sticker that said "Proud Parent of an Average Student" or "My Daughter Passed to the Next Grade at Fremont High"?

Don't get me wrong. All parents look for ways to give their children a little extra edge in life. There's nothing wrong with that. I confess I've done it myself. I bought my son an encyclopedia for his second birthday. He ate volume "C." I sent my children to computer camp. They got poison ivy in their disc drive. And as for early music lessons, you should have seen them on the piano

. . . and on the coffee table . . . and on the bookshelves . . . and on the . . .

When you get right down to it, though, don't children meet with the pressure to compete in life soon enough? Perhaps we should put away that "Toddler's Guide to the Stock Market" for just a few more years. Maybe we should let that future football star enjoy his first steps before we start training him to run those 60-yard touchdowns. After all, childhood is like a good movie. We can fast-forward our way through it, but if we do, we'll end up missing all the best parts.

"Worth thousands"   "Worth millions"   "Worth the sacrifice of God's only begotten Son, Jesus"

▸▸▸19◂◂◂

MY FATHER'S TREASURES

My father was a collector—not of Hummel figures or rare coins but of secondhand "treasures." A secondhand store to my father was like a telephone booth to a teenager. It was virtually impossible for him to pass one without stopping in for an hour or two.

Over the years Dad brought home many sorts of knickknacks—most of which had been knicked and knacked beyond recognition. He'd bring home cracked dishes, leaky vases, and statues that were missing more body parts than Venus de Milo. Dad never let the current condition of an object deter him from purchasing it. He had the talent of looking past its apparent worth and envisioning what it could become with a little glue, a little paint, and a lot of faith.

Not all the treasures Dad brought home were broken. Many of them were mere discards—seemingly worthless items that others had passed over.

I'll never forget the time he was rummaging through a box at a local thrift store and came across the perfect mate to an old bookend he had at home. Hardly believing his good fortune, he rushed home to show my mother the near-miraculous find. Mom had been after him for years to toss out his useless, old bookend. Now she was going to have to admit he'd been right in hanging on to it for so long. He couldn't wait to see the look on her face. Instead of being thrilled with his find, however, my mother simply made a confession: the bookend Dad had just paid two dollars for *was* his old bookend. She had given it away to that particular charity three months earlier.

Everyone, including my father, got a good laugh, but the incident didn't alter Dad's shopping habits one bit. He continued his regular treasure hunts at local thrift shops, bringing home the broken, the rusted, the seemingly worthless. He'd paint over their chips and sand off their scratches. Then, after doing whatever it took to make them whole again, he'd give them a place of honor in the house—either on the coffee table or on the shelf above the sofa. Proudly, he'd set them right next to the more expensive department store items. Not only could no one tell the difference, but we received more compliments on Dad's "treasures" than on anything else.

Aren't you glad that when our Heavenly Father looked down at us, He didn't see worthless discards but hidden treasures?